TOP 10 FASTEST

Planes

SHERRY HOWARD

Rourke Educational Media
A Division of Carson Dellosa Education
rourkeeducationalmedia.com

ROURKE'S **SCHOOL to HOME** CONNECTIONS

BEFORE AND DURING READING ACTIVITIES

Before Reading: *Building Background Knowledge and Vocabulary*

Building background knowledge can help children process new information and build upon what they already know. Before reading a book, it is important to tap into what children already know about the topic. This will help them develop their vocabulary and increase their reading comprehension.

Questions and Activities to Build Background Knowledge:

1. Look at the front cover of the book and read the title. What do you think this book will be about?
2. What do you already know about this topic?
3. Take a book walk and skim the pages. Look at the table of contents, photographs, captions, and bold words. Did these text features give you any information or predictions about what you will read in this book?

Vocabulary: *Vocabulary Is Key to Reading Comprehension*

Use the following directions to prompt a conversation about each word.

- Read the vocabulary words.
- What comes to mind when you see each word?
- What do you think each word means?

Vocabulary Words:

- *altitude*
- *manned*
- *marvels*
- *nuclear*
- *pillar*
- *stealth*

During Reading: *Reading for Meaning and Understanding*

To achieve deep comprehension of a book, children are encouraged to use close reading strategies. During reading, it is important to have children stop and make connections. These connections result in deeper analysis and understanding of a book.

Close Reading a Text

During reading, have children stop and talk about the following:

- Any confusing parts
- Any unknown words
- Text to text, text to self, text to world connections
- The main idea in each chapter or heading

Encourage children to use context clues to determine the meaning of any unknown words. These strategies will help children learn to analyze the text more thoroughly as they read.

When you are finished reading this book, turn to the next-to-last page for **After Reading Questions** and an **Activity**.

Table of Contents

First, Fast, Fastest

The Wright brothers had a goal. They wanted to fly. So they built a plane. And they flew!

Their plane stayed in the air for 12 seconds in 1903.

Planes became the fastest way to travel. Soon it was a race to be the fastest in the sky. The fastest planes set records.

Most of the world's fastest planes are used by militaries. They carry weapons. They spy from the sky.

F-111 Aardvark

This plane flew faster than the speed of sound. This is called *supersonic* speed.

Bell X-2 Starbuster

This was a research plane. It was powered by rockets. One pilot flew almost three times the speed of sound!

Research planes test conditions at high speeds. They test how pilots handle heights.

North American X-15

The world's first space plane flew more than six times the speed of sound. It holds the world record for the fastest **manned** aircraft.

manned (mand): having a human crew

It was first flown in 1959. It had to be carried up and dropped.

XB-70 Valkyrie

This plane was built to escape a **nuclear** bomb blast. Only two of these planes were ever built.

nuclear (NOO-klee-ur): of or relating to the energy created by the splitting of atoms

U.S. AIR FORCE

Mikoyan MiG-25 Foxbat

This plane was built to stop United States aircraft during the Cold War. It is one of the fastest supersonic planes ever built.

During the Cold War, relations between the Soviet Union and the U.S. were tense. Both had nuclear bombs. Both explored space.

Lockheed YF-12

This plane carried three missiles. It set several speed and **altitude** records. Only three were built.

10 **altitude** (AL-ti-tood): height above the ground

U.S. AIR FORCE

Lockheed SR-71 Blackbird

This plane was developed in secret. It could outfly enemy missiles. **Stealth** technology made it hard for enemies to track.

10 **stealth** (stelth): silent, secret, and cautious

The Blackbird was so fast that the air in front of it built up pressure. The air got hotter. Heat makes metal expand, so the plane's pieces had to be small.

McDonnell Douglas F-15 Eagle

This aircraft is a **pillar** of the U.S. military. It flies more than twice the speed of sound.

10 **pillar** (PIL-ur): something or someone that is relied upon

More than a thousand of these planes have been built. They are used by the U.S. and sold to other countries.

Mikoyan MiG-31 Foxhound

This plane has supersonic speed at any altitude. It was built to take out enemy aircraft.

23
38

Sukhoi Su-27

This fighter plane can travel at twice the speed of sound. It carries missiles, bombs, and guns.

58

The world's fastest planes are engineering **marvels**. What will engineers come up with next?

marvels (MAHR-vuhls): wonderful or astonishing people or things

Memory Game

Look at the pictures. What do you remember reading on the pages where each image appeared?

Index

After Reading Questions

1. Which plane has supersonic speed at any altitude?
2. Which plane was built to escape the blast of a nuclear bomb?
3. Which plane does the U.S. military rely on?
4. How long did the Wright brothers' first flight last?
5. Which plane has stealth technology?

Activity

Which plane interests you most? Using books and the internet, research that plane further. What more can you learn about who developed the plane and how it is used? Write a story about piloting that plane.

About the Author

Sherry Howard has flown in commercial aircraft and little tiny planes. She'd prefer not to fly at supersonic speed. She'd rather keep her feet planted on the bluegrass of Kentucky.

www.rourkeeducationalmedia.com

PHOTO CREDITS: Cover, pages 1, 10-1, 12-13, 18-19, 20-21, 30: ©NASA; pages 4-5: ©Elenarts; pages 6-7: ©Jorge Villalba; pages 8-9, 30: ©Thor Jorgen Udvang; pages 14-15: ©US Gov; pages 16-17, 22-23, 24-25, 30: ©vaalaa; pages 26-27, 30: ©Jason Wells; pages 28-29; ©iurii

Edited by: Kim Thompson
Cover and Interior design by: Kathy Walsh

Library of Congress PCN Data

Planes / Sherry Howard
(Top Ten Fastest)
ISBN 978-1-73161-461-2 (hardcover)
ISBN 978-1-73161-262-5 (soft cover)
ISBN 978-1-73161-566-4 (e-Book)
ISBN 978-1-73161-671-5 (ePub)
Library of Congress Control Number: 2019932368

Rourke Educational Media
Printed in the United States of America,
North Mankato, Minnesota